~~the~~ ~~incidenta~~
THE ARCHITECTURE OF TASTE

THE ARCHITECTURE OF TASTE

PIERRE HERMÉ

WITH SAVINIEN CARACOSTEA
AND SANFORD KWINTER

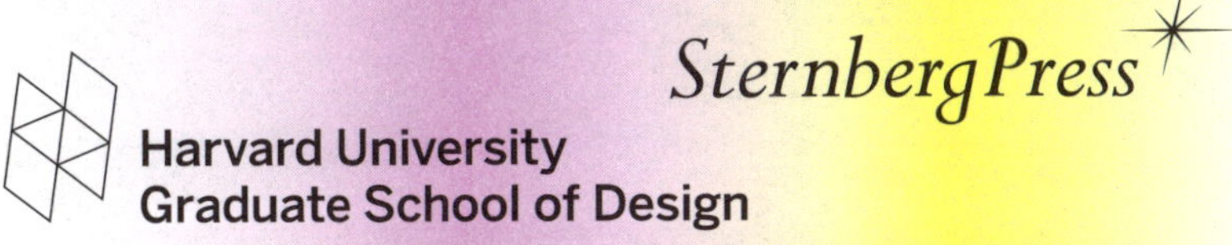

Sternberg Press

Harvard University
Graduate School of Design

Created by   SAVINIEN CARACOSTEA
Hosted by   MOHSEN MOSTAFAVI
Chaired by   SANFORD KWINTER
Produced by   SHANTEL BLAKELY
Edited by   JENNIFER SIGLER
                  LEAH WHITMAN-SALKIN
Translated by   CHARLES PENWARDEN
Designed by   ÅBÄKE
Printed by   PRINTON, ESTONIA
Published by   HARVARD UNIVERSITY
                  GRADUATE SCHOOL OF DESIGN
                  STERNBERG PRESS

November 27, 2012
Piper Auditorium, Gund Hall
Harvard University Graduate School of Design
Cambridge, Massachusetts, USA

Piper Auditorium — 6:30 P.M.
(The auditorium is an expansive yet intimate space. In the front half of the room, long tables covered in white linens are arranged in neat stripes, perpendicular to the stage; in the back half, rows of stepped seating overlook the banquet tables below. Sanford Kwinter and Pierre Hermé chat off to the side as guests file in. Lights dim. The audience is seated.)

SAVINIEN CARACOSTEA   Good evening. It is my pleasure to introduce the esteemed pastry chef Pierre Hermé. As a student of both architecture and pastry, I have observed many parallels between the two fields — particularly in that ready-to-eat confections, like built architectural works, tend to conceal the complex processes that bring them into being. *(Pause.)* Recently, and largely because of the work of chefs like Pierre Hermé, the edible has been popularized

SAVINIEN CARACOSTEA

as a medium of cultural expression and invention. In the tradition of historic projects that reveal food's relationship to other arts — like the manifesto by the celebrated 19th-century pastry chef Antonin Carême, which stated that "the most noble of all the arts is architecture, and its greatest manifestation is the art of the pastry chef," and F. T. Marinetti's avant-garde *Futurist Cookbook* from the 1930s, in which the artist composed sensorial poetry through food — Hermé's work introduces a cross-disciplinary notion of cooking, or an "architecture of taste." One of the few chefs who mention architecture when describing their creative processes, Pierre Hermé takes a rigorous, pragmatic, and intuitive approach to his work. Within his discipline, he addresses larger design issues concerning not simply form, but process, technique, and sensory experience. (*Pause.*) Please join me in welcoming Pierre Hermé.

THE INCIDENTS

PIERRE HERMÉ Good evening, ladies and gentlemen. I will start by explaining the way I work and how I create pastries. People often ask me where my ideas come from. My ideas come mainly from my desires. My desires are generated in different ways—by what I taste, what I read, who I talk to. I don't need to make things in three dimensions in order to imagine them; on the contrary, I build maquettes in my head. I imagine flavors, sensations, textures—and all the emotions they provide. Later, to "fix" these ideas, and to convey them to the pastry chefs who will execute them, I write them out as recipes. As I compose a recipe, I create what I call a "taste scenario." I visualize putting the pastry in my mouth, and imagine what happens first, second, third, and what may surprise. I plan these events from the outset. (*Pause.*) Everything starts with taste; form comes much later. I make drawings not to depict the appearance of a pastry, but to clarify the proportions of the different components. Then I start writing. I only start writing when I know what result I want to achieve.

INFINIMENT CITRON
[IDENTIFICATION OF TASTE]

(*With the textures of the pâte sablée
and meringue establishing themselves
as constants, a lemon aroma emerges.*)

PIERRE HERMÉ   Four cakes sit in front of each of you.
The first, with the slice of lemon, is the
Infiniment Citron. Please remove the slice of
lemon and take a bite from the top, straight
through to the bottom of the cake. Infiniment
Citron is made of a lemon pâte sablée, lemon
cream, lemon gelée and candied lemon, lemon
flesh, lemon Chantilly, and is topped with
lemon meringue and white chocolate lemon
slices. (*Pause.*) In my work, I often develop
a single taste and try to intensify it. When I
focus on one specific flavor, I call it *Infiniment*
[infinitely]. This is how I express my very
personal idealization of a particular taste,
whether it's vanilla, caramel, or in this case,
lemon. I've also started working on coffee.
(*Pause.*) My process always starts with trying
to understand the components, and searching
the world for the finest ingredients. For the
Infiniment Citron, I went to Italy to meet
lemon growers. It is vital that my supplies are
consistent and provided by suppliers who I
have worked with to identify the right varietals
and specifications. Then, I asked myself: what
is interesting about lemon? It is the acidity,
the bitterness, and the distinctive aroma.
(*Pause.*) A particular taste can be expressed or

(*The intrinsic tartness of the lemon
slowly gives way to bitterness, while
the pâte sablée and meringue textures
persist.*)

(*The bitterness transitions into
acidity, then back to bitterness,
then back to acidity.*)

(*Finally, the aroma of the lemon
comes back and reconnects with
the pâte sablée and meringue.*)

PIERRE HERMÉ reinterpreted through several kinds of pastry. I start with one interpretation, which becomes 10, then 100. For instance, I've created a whole family based on the Infiniment Citron taste. Each creation is unique. For some, I focused on lemon's acidity; for others, on its tartness; for others, on the balance between bitterness and acidity. These are not variations; for each creation, the taste is totally reinterpreted. Even though these products involve the same flavors, the materials differ and they are combined in unique ways. Making a cake is not the same thing as making ice cream or a chocolate bonbon or a croissant. Each calls for a genuine reinterpretation. In each of these iterations, the taste scenario changes, but the harmony of ingredients remains the same. Each product has its own personality. In the one you are tasting now, there is a contrast of textures; in the different parts of your mouth you can feel the various dimensions of the lemon. It's a very simple cake; it attempts to make the taste of lemon as precise as it can be. When you bite through the entire cross section of the pastry, you can understand what it means to highlight a single taste. There is nothing but lemon in this pastry.

SAVINIEN CARACOSTEA You work to understand the ingredients and to deconstruct and identify their traits, which allows you to play with them and make them your own. The holographic rendition we are tasting tonight is just one of your twists on the nuances of lemon. The Infiniment collections highlight flavors that are common but often have rich forgotten histories. Through your renditions, you animate these flavors and histories by going back to their origins. Taste then becomes a spatial medium, capable of moving us through a constructed sequence of intimate experiences, all sparked by the connection between flavor and memory. Here, your work begins to cross the classical boundaries between disciplines. The next pastry articulates very clearly the dimensions of taste you are working with.

<u>YASAMINE</u>
[DIMENSIONS OF TASTE]

(The macaron biscuit crumbles under the bite. The floral and bitter notes of the candied grapefruit and jasmine are present.)

(The floral and fruity notes of the fresh mango, which has been seasoned with ginger and lemon, now emerge. The crispiness of the biscuit persists.)

PIERRE HERMÉ   The second creation I am inviting you to taste, Yasamine, looks like a big macaron. It is a macaron biscuit with jasmine cream. It's made with an infusion of jasmine tea—a very exceptional tea—along with pieces of fresh mango, seasoned with lemon and ginger and bits of candied grapefruit peel. Grapefruit is bitter, and I also classify jasmine in the bitter category. Mango is very fruity and exuberant, which introduces a fresh note. (*Pause.*) When I started to plan this pastry, I had a clear idea in my mind; I knew exactly what I wanted to achieve. But our first trials were unsuccessful; I was not able to produce what I had in mind. So I decided to put the project aside for about a year. During that time, I thought about the techniques and ingredients that would best translate my idea. (*Pause.*) I like to reinterpret classic pastries. The macaron is a good example. I have worked on the macaron for over 25 years. When I learned how to make macarons in 1976, they typically consisted of two biscuits stuck together with a tiny bit of jam. I found them very sweet and lacking a complexity of flavor. I didn't like macarons!

SANFORD KWINTER   I want to start where most people start with Pierre Hermé's pastries — with the macaron. In a recent book called *The Omnivorous Mind*, John Allen, a cognitive neuroscientist, makes the case for why crispiness has assumed such importance as a provocative trait in the universe of eatable things. Did crispiness have as its original purpose to render insects delectable to early humans who were not fully equipped to hunt for meat? Insects are still highly valued in many cultures, and form part of the essential diets of various civilizations. Allen further asks if raw fruits and vegetables that snap when bitten into derive their desirability from their cells, which are still

PIERRE HERMÉ   But I thought that maybe one could juxtapose
two creams, two fillings, to produce successive
flavors. When you mix everything into a single
cream you don't get the same effect as you can
with two separate fillings. Take, for example,
the Ispahan jam. In order to reinterpret the
Ispahan flavors, I created a jam with two
layers, litchi-rose and raspberry. We tell clients
to mix the two layers themselves. If we mixed
the two when making the jam, the perception
of the tastes would be fundamentally different.

SANFORD KWINTER plumped with water, and which signify freshness. Might crispiness be said to guide our senses to high-yield places in our surrounding ecology? (*Pause.*) I am delighted to have a chef at my side to ask about crispiness and about the importance of the Maillard reaction. The Maillard reaction accounts for just about all the effects of aromatic browning, a process by which an ingredient's amino acids and sugars react in such a way that the surface dehydrates, as in grilling and roasting. Everything delicious about food is derived from the Maillard reaction. Was it the Maillard reaction that established the definitive, positive association of crispiness with the intense release of flavor compounds associated with controlled dry cooking (baking)? What role has the macaron played in redefining and repopularizing crispiness? It deploys crispiness in a complex and subtle way, where a crust, a shell, plays the role of counterpoint to the flowing sensation of softness and the *moelleux*—a marvelous word that in English means pliability, wetness, chewiness. The macaron has a brittle, dry type of crispiness—delicate, but structurally firm.

PIERRE HERMÉ   The register of crispiness can be expressed in many different ways. There is of course the immediate crispiness of a brioche, a croissant, or a macaron. There is a different crispiness in certain cakes made with crushed wafers — a crispiness you can express with bits of chocolate. But I think that you're talking about the relation between the apparent freshness of a baked product and its intrinsic crispiness. When you see something that looks crispy, it's appetizing — it's appealing. It makes you want it. Many pastries express this immediate crispiness, whether a choux pastry, an éclair, or a gâteau St. Honoré. Others, like Émotion Délicieux, are registered as supple, a bit soft, deliberately uncrispy. (*Pause.*) When I started making macarons, I realized that what gives them their taste is the filling. So I created fillings with very concentrated tastes, and increased the proportion of filling to biscuit. While I was head pastry chef at Fauchon in the early 1980s, I introduced simple flavors that are now classic — lemon, pistachio, rose — and I got away from the flavors you found everywhere else, like raspberry, vanilla, chocolate, and coffee. Later, in the mid-1990s,

(The fruitiness of the mango can now be identified. As it takes over, a slight acidity becomes perceptible.)

(The jasmine returns to the constant crispiness of the biscuit.)

PIERRE HERMÉ   I thought: why not create more inventive combinations of flavors for macarons, like I do for my pastries? So I began to use the macaron as a simpler and more direct expression of the kinds of flavor pairings I created for my more complex pastries. (*Pause.*) The macarons, like all my work, are about the construction of taste. I also put crispiness and crunchiness inside the macarons—bits of hazelnuts, tiny pieces of dehydrated olives. If these olive pieces were to be mixed directly with the cream, they would give the cream a salty taste; instead, three little bits of olive placed on top of each macaron impart only a slight salty edge. On the other hand, when you taste an Infiniment Cassis macaron, you first taste the black currant cream, but then, suddenly, three little black currants release their acidic juice, surprise the mouth, and, for me, give pleasure. These little spurts of acidity heighten the taste and produce an unexpected sensation. (*Pause.*) As you taste the Yasamine macaron this evening, you discover that each mouthful is different. Each mouthful is a surprise.

SANFORD KWINTER The unexpected, the surprise, was a central part of large dinners in ancient Rome. The Romans viewed these events as opportunities for pulling gags, making jokes in poor taste — like food that moved. Live animals were buried inside cooked animals that would suddenly start to crawl across the table. Pranks like these were an integral part of those meals. I would suggest that you do something similar in your pastries: you orchestrate little surprises with sudden movements, transitions, transformations that force uncanny accommodations on us. It's a form of hacking, *hacking the brain* ...

PIERRE HERMÉ   The word "hacking" is right. I like flavors to
appear as if by chance, unexpectedly: all of
a sudden, a touch of acidity, a hint of salt or
sugar. This is not something I do consciously;
it comes from responding to my own desires.

SAVINIEN CARACOSTEA This element of surprise brings a
fourth dimension to your scripting
of pastry. The notion of time in your
work reinforces the feeling of space.
In the next pastry, the vertical
configuration of the components,
like a geological cut, stresses the
importance of sequence — in both time
and space — in the tasting experience.

PLAISIR SUCRÉ
[SPATIALIZATION OF TASTE]

(*The flavor is immediately
discernible: milk chocolate and
hazelnut. It will be consistent
throughout. The top layer of
chocolate crunches as it is
bitten into.*)

PIERRE HERMÉ   The next pastry is the milk chocolate Plaisir Sucré. Be careful not to eat the little pastel on top. (*Pause.*) If we are talking about the architecture of taste, this pastry is a very good example. It expresses several sensations; one is based on a familiar taste combination: milk chocolate and hazelnuts. But this is not any milk chocolate, and these are not any hazelnuts. These are hazelnuts from Piedmont, which is where you find the best hazelnuts in the world. The milk chocolate has a cacao content of 45 percent, which is very high for milk chocolate. I devised it with our supplier. It is a unique, exclusive product. (*Pause.*) Plaisir Sucré is a typical example of

(*From the crunchiness, the softness of the ganache emerges.*)

(*The softness gives way to crispiness, then unctuousness.*)

PIERRE HERMÉ an extremely structured pastry. It offers a multitude of sensations and textures at once: crispiness, crunchiness, brittleness, chewiness, and creaminess. I may have forgotten some, but it offers virtually all the textures you can imagine. (*Pause.*) Form conditions the tasting experience. When the shape of a chocolate confection changes, the taste perception does too. I use three forms when constructing chocolates. The first, for ganaches, is fairly long, not very wide, and quite thick. When you bite into the chocolate you experience an agreeable sensation; a smooth, velvety sensation. There is also a slightly wider format, with equal length and thickness, which I tend to use for pralines. It's a more gourmand format. Finally, there is a flatter format, three-by-three centimeters, which is half as thick. I use it for more delicate creations. There, too, the form enhances different sensations and allows me to combine ingredients in various ways. When working in the realm of chocolate, I add flavors like lemon, raspberry, pepper, caramel, and praline. But the tastes of these ingredients are transient. (*Pause.*) When you eat a chocolate bonbon, you taste the chocolate

*(The cracking of the hazelnut pieces
end the bite, yet the unctuous
quality endures alongside the milk
chocolate and hazelnut flavors.)*

SAVINIEN CARACOSTEA   The degree of attention you give
to your chocolates and pastries
causes them to consume us as we
consume them. The renewed cultural
interest in the culinary reveals
a world that cannot be accurately
communicated through images,
but through craft that triggers
experiences and emotions. Pastries
can be thought of as a very cinematic
food. Constructed and entertaining,
they are little spectacles meant
to finish off a meal, or offer a
pleasant break during the day. Your
creations show us that each bite can
contain a very thoughtful montage
of distinct layers and textures

PIERRE HERMÉ first, then you experience the ingredient it is combined with, and at the end, the chocolate impression lingers. I like to finish with chocolate, not with the complimentary ingredient. (*Pause.*) The architecture of taste is this evening's theme, and this is precisely what I have just been talking about: the construction of taste.

SAVINIEN CARACOSTEA that affect us directly through
our experience of eating them.
Time seems to dilate when eating a
pastry, as if, like the frames of a
filmstrip, we experience flavor 24
times a second. In this cinematic
realm, pastries are buildings just
as buildings are pastries. Ever since
hunting scenes were painted on the
undulating walls of Paleolithic caves,
sequenced almost like cinematic
narratives, art and architecture,
when combined, have often turned to
a more primal medium — the edible —
to come to life. The classic fairy
tale "Hansel and Gretel" describes
the house that is eaten, but that
also eats. Salvador Dalí, when
describing art nouveau architecture
as "terrifying and comestible,"
pointed to the surrealist ambiguity
of the built environment and
consumption — buildings are both
edible and carnivorous, as we enter
the mouth of the cave.

SAVINIEN CARACOSTEA   The last pastry that you selected
for us is as close a manifestation of
cinema as I have ever experienced in
food. It is a deconstructed creation,
liberated from the traditional
constraints of pastry.

ÉMOTION DÉLICIEUX
[TRANSCENDING THE REAL]

(*The grapefruit blends with the
sharp flavor of the wasabi, but
also expresses its own bitterness.*)

PIERRE HERMÉ   Yes, the pastry we are going to conclude with
is rather surprising, and a bit disorienting.
This is Émotion Délicieux, which has a base of
wasabi and yuzu jelly, bits of fresh and candied
grapefruit, a mascarpone cream, and green tea
marshmallow pieces on top. It should be eaten
with a spoon. It is very important to go from
the top to the bottom with the spoon — to
taste everything at the same time. Otherwise,
I can promise unpleasant reactions. (*Pause.*)
I initiated this construction in 2006. At that
time I was a bit bored with the constraints of a
cake, because they imposed many limitations
on the compositions I could imagine. The
format of a cake requires that it support itself,
that it can stand for several hours in the shop
display, and that one can then bring it home
and keep it for another few hours in the

SANFORD KWINTER Into what other contexts — such as the unique and fantastic performance we are collectively experiencing in which you are delivering a "lecture de pâtisserie" — can the disciplined ingestion of constructed foodstuffs be placed? What other contexts push beyond the pleasure element alone, and engage the larger complex of sensations and experience that you're interested in? Could you envisage giving food a social, perhaps even political, role by staging its consumption in different ways? There seems no reason why pastry has to be eaten with tea or in the afternoon or at home after dinner. Would you like to speculate on some of the contexts you might imagine creating for eating pastry?

PIERRE HERMÉ fridge before eating it. But I wanted to make creations with more supple compositions. This pastry, then, is a kind of deconstruction of a cake; I have turned a cake into something else.

PIERRE HERMÉ That's an interesting suggestion. It's something worth pursuing. I can certainly imagine staging pastry in a different way, yes.

SANFORD KWINTER   Let it be pointed out that Monsieur Hermé reflexively employs the phrase *mettre en scène* — to stage a scene — when he talks about experiencing a pastry. I know this is not just because we've been talking about it as a film …

(*The mustardy, spicy wasabi emerges violently and sends us back to the grapefruit.*)

PIERRE HERMÉ   One of the pastries you ate earlier tonight,
Plaisir Sucré, is also served in a larger iteration,
designed for sharing; it is called La Cerise sur
le Gâteau [the Cherry on the Cake]. It was
my first "designed" pastry, dating from 1993.
I asked an industrial designer, Yan Pennor's,
to design a cake that a pastry chef could
never imagine, one with a more ceremonial
presentation. The product we created looked
like a thin slice of cake with a glassy cherry
on top and very minimal gold notches along
the edges. To slice this cake, you have to lay
it on its side and cut along the notches. The
cake is further theatricalized by its triangular
box, which folds open like a flower. Both
the packaging and the cake were designed
together, expanding the experience of the
cake to include its display and the ritual of its
cutting. It is the only cake that I have made
with a designer.

SANFORD KWINTER   I want now to coax you to venture over to our
territory a bit, or at any rate, to engage our
language. Architecture, like many formal arts,
is haunted by classicism. We often repudiate
classicism and its oppressive forms, but we also
go back to them with a certain regularity as a

PIERRE HERMÉ Since most of the people here are interested in architecture and design, there is a question that must be nagging at you. In all pastries, ice creams, sorbets, bonbons, and chocolates, taste is interpreted in a different way, but there is a guiding thread, which we could call "style." My style is based on essence—about getting to the essential. I make pastries appetizing with only the essential materials I've used to compose them. Their look expresses their composition, suggests their narrative. What can one say about appearance? People are often tempted to add ornament. That, I can tell you, is a big temptation. But because I know precisely what I want to express, I find it easy to dismiss that temptation. Of course there are some exceptions. With the Ispahan, for instance, the decorative rose petal brings such a poetic touch—I couldn't resist.

SANFORD KWINTER   ritual of simplification or recalibration. A great deal of culinary culture since the 1970s consists of a repudiation of the principles of classicism and an affirmation of innovation. I'd say you're part of that tradition. Sometimes it has to do with innovation for its own sake. You took the inherited idea of a gâteau (you often speak of going beyond the assumptions of the classic cake — *au-delà du gâteau*), and in many ways affect to renounce it. Where does your own anti-classicism stand in relation to the discourse of modern culinary design and to current forms of practice?

(The acidity of the grapefruit is reinforced by the yuzu.)

PIERRE HERMÉ If you want to be creative you have to know
the classics. I know all the classics and the
thousands of ways of interpreting them. What I
learned during my apprenticeship with Gaston
Lenôtre, the first chef to open an upscale
pastry chain in Paris, had a profound effect on
me. It forms the real base of my know-how,
and I still draw on it today. It took me years
to be able to distance myself from what I had
learned from Lenôtre, to be able to draw on
it while developing my own style, creating my
own desires. (*Pause.*) In the world of cuisine

PIERRE HERMÉ   there are movements. There was a movement
called Nouvelle Cuisine in the 1970s and
1980s. Nouvelle Cuisine signaled the moment
when dishes became autonomous—we went
from dishes served for *x* number of people
to dishes served on individual plates. Sauces
and preparations in general were given a
lighter touch. Cooking methods moved toward
steaming. As with all culinary movements,
there were people who initiated trends and
movements and those who followed. Nouvelle
Cuisine was a great moment of culinary
creativity. When the movement started
running out of steam, people turned toward
more classical traditions, but continued to
bring in ideas from Nouvelle Cuisine. It wasn't
a question of turning back the clock. (*Pause.*)
After that came the fusion cuisine movement,
which incorporated a certain number of new
ideas, new mixes, that transgressed classical
techniques. That was followed by another
movement initiated by Spanish chefs, Ferran
Adrià in particular, called molecular cuisine.
It focused on technological innovations and
new forms of preparation. In recent years
there has been a reaction against this kind

SANFORD KWINTER   In the end, do you see your particular direction
as a kind of a modernism or a kind of classicism?

PIERRE HERMÉ   of cuisine, but there's no denying that this period enriched traditional cuisine. (*Pause.*) With every creative movement, classical cooking is enhanced by new contributions, and never returns completely to where it started. For me, creativity in pastry is not incompatible with traditional know-how. On the contrary, I apply historical concepts, but with technical innovations and new ingredients. There is perpetual movement.

PIERRE HERMÉ   It's difficult for me to answer that question, because what I make is part of who I am; it's something that comes from me. It's something that brings pleasure. And through what I do, through the emotions I structure and organize, I create pleasure. Yet when I imagine pastries, I am not making them for someone in particular. I make them to please all those who taste them. If I am asked to make a cake for children, I am incapable of doing so. However, if you come to see me and you tell me that you want a cake that is like this and like that,

SAVINIEN CARACOSTEA Making a custom cake for an individual is an interesting idea. I have often thought of your pastries as characters themselves, with their own narratives evolving from season to season. As one pans across the display case in your boutiques, the abstract forms of the pastries are further personified by names such as "Ispahan" and "Mogador," referencing an atlas of distant geographies anchored in our collective imaginary. Together, they are like frames from a proto-cinematic film in which each static confection suggests movement and our minds interpolate narratives between them. In this regard, it's very revealing that you call your collections "fetishes."

PIERRE HERMÉ   with this kind of taste, I am perfectly capable
of making a unique creation, just for you, based
on what you express. I do that for a few clients.

PIERRE HERMÉ   What I call a "fetish" is an exploration of
a product or form through all its facets or
flavor associations. (*Pause.*) To come back to

(*Soft matcha marshmallows introduce
a new texture, keeping the experience
in motion.*)

PIERRE HERMÉ the origin of my ideas, about 20 years ago
I was in Italy, in Liguria, and I tasted pastries
made with olive oil. That's when I discovered
the use of olive oil in pastry. What does olive
oil do in a biscuit or a cake? It imparts a much
softer texture than butter; it's completely
different. That experience set off a desire to
use olive oil, and the first pastry I made with
olive oil was a macaron. In the meantime,
I had discovered an olive oil in Tuscany with
vanilla aromas. I found it so interesting that
I made a macaron with olive oil and vanilla.
This is all part of a process fueled by my
curiosity, by the things I taste, by experiences
and encounters—and that is really where
my creations come from. In general, I am
interested in all kinds of tastes—the tastes
that people tell me are very good and those
that are not very good. If you want to know
what is good, you have to taste what is not
good so you can establish a scale of values.
I am very curious and I taste everything that
comes before my nose. I also smell everything.
These habits help me create a mental library
that I can use to create and imagine taste
scenarios. (*Pause.*) I want to show you a book;

PIERRE HERMÉ   it's a book I published titled *Au coeur du goût*. It's a work I did with a nose, a perfumer, because our creative processes are very similar. In this book you have both the great classical harmonies of pastry and the great harmonies of perfumery, which I reinterpreted based on the descriptions given to me by Jean-Michel Duriez, my coauthor, the nose. The idea of the book is not simply to describe the taste of perfume, but to go to the heart of taste. There are also perfumes — great, well-known perfumes — that we interpreted; notably Femme by Rochas, the main notes of which are peach and cumin. So I made a tart with peaches, rose, and cumin, with pâte brisée, rose-flavored almond cream, and fresh peaches, sprinkled with cumin sugar. We also worked on what in perfumery is called *enfleurage* — putting a fat-based element in contact with another so that it absorbs its fragrance. For example, we made a melon-flavored madeleine that didn't contain a gram of melon; its flavor was entirely generated through contact between the butter and melon. Of course, there are recipes, but there is above all this exchange between the two of us — the perfumer and pastry chef.

SANFORD KWINTER   So, do pastries have to be sweet?

SANFORD KWINTER   A marvelous, and exquisitely modern answer.

PIERRE HERMÉ   In the dessert you are now tasting there is a wasabi and yuzu jelly. I went to visit a wasabi producer in Japan and when I tasted the fresh roots, straight from the earth, I realized that the first centimeters, the ones deepest in the earth, are very sweet. That discovery prompted me to introduce another sensation into my world of pastry, because wasabi is neither savory nor sweet, neither bitter nor acidic. I call it mustardy, because it produces a sensation that is also produced by mustard or horseradish. This flavor is offset by acidity and bitterness, so it interacts well with the other components. Of course there is sweetness, but it's not very sweet. It's a bit disturbing — that's why I want you to taste it last. I like using ingredients taken from the savory universe, not for the effect, but to create different flavor combinations.

PIERRE HERMÉ   That's a good question. I always say that the most important thing about sugar is salt.

SANFORD KWINTER The one important tendency you haven't yet told us about has to do with the moment when cooking began to target the emotions, began to target memory, and through these to target the soul and the movements of the soul. For example, you speak a great deal about surprises and the way you use these to startle the senses and compel them into a moment of reorganization. The impression generated by the mixing of the grapefruit and the wasabi, while mediated by a mild but somewhat sweet and tart citrus taste, was for me absolutely astonishing and I can

PIERRE HERMÉ   Salt puts sugar on a pedestal. More generally, it's a question of balance between sweetness, acidity, bitterness, and salt. For example, there is a classic pastry called mille-feuille; you call it a Napoleon. It's a pastry with very little sugar. The puff pastry is always savory, only the cream is sweet, and so it makes a very nice salty-sweet balance. In the classic mille-feuille, you include a layer of icing that is pure sugar, which creates an asynchronous effect. The sugar isn't inside, it is on top — quite an interesting organization. I envy the person who invented the mille-feuille.

SANFORD KWINTER only surmise what types of dreams it will stir in me tonight. Flavors are memories; they are evocations; they are the very motivations in our cells — and they induce reorganization processes that place us ever more firmly in our worlds. The reason we brought pastries to the lecture hall was to affect the audience, and I am affected! (*Pause.*) Tonight, Monsieur Hermé laid out a clear case for the assertion that we eat with our brains. This insight is one shared by more and more chefs today, particularly among the greatest culinary innovators; they seem to understand that to prepare food is to orchestrate — to trigger and set into motion — an incredible syllabus of moods, chains of ideas, memories, sensations ...

SAVINIEN CARACOSTEA It also renews the importance of the body; it brings our visually dominant culture literally back to its other senses.

SANFORD KWINTER I am said to be the theorist, and I recognize that in many ways what Monsieur Hermé is doing is laying out the foundations of a theory of the architecture of taste. To take the basic framework of the "counterpoint," upon which

SANFORD KWINTER

so many of the effects you create are based, is to be reminded of the earliest forms of Western musical organization that led to the astounding complexity of what we are able to do with sound today. The counterpoint techniques support Savinien's initial suggestion tonight that in your hands a pastry has a tendency to become cinema, an orchestration or mise-en-scène of sensations that assumes the structure of a script. (*Pause.*) Now, if I may jump to a more difficult speculation: I am thinking of the important 20th-century composer Karlheinz Stockhausen who claimed that we humans are literally transistors because we continually receive organized signals that change and modify us; tones actually enter and attack us and change us, both directly and physically and via neurochemical pathways.
In so many ways I see in this exactly what you do: You assemble these materials and present them to our senses — we ingest the pastries and are literally modified by them. You induce these uncanny yet determined effects upon us. (*Pause.*) The work you do consists of organizing matter. When we spoke a few weeks ago, you repeated frequently, "Yes, we're going to send the matière première to New York." For me this

SANFORD KWINTER expression was a poignant evocation because it alluded to a transformation, to the alchemy that you effectuate first in the kitchen as you assemble or design the object, as you invest the "primary" stuff with process. But there is the necessary moment of transfer: when the object enters us and literally recomposes us, activates our nervous system and transforms the pathways of sensation and chemistry in our bodies, associating and dissociating memory and sensation. This is a prominent dream of architects and artists today who seek to do exactly what you do. (*Pause.*) Cher Pierre, to you and to your remarkable team, allow me on behalf of all of us to thank you for an extraordinary night, a night we will remember.

PIERRE HERMÉ Thank you.

<u>APPENDIX 1</u>

<u>APPENDIX 1</u>

MAISON

PIERRE HERMÉ

12 RUE FORTUNY   PARIS 17ᵉ

<u>INFINIMENT CITRON</u> (p. 12)

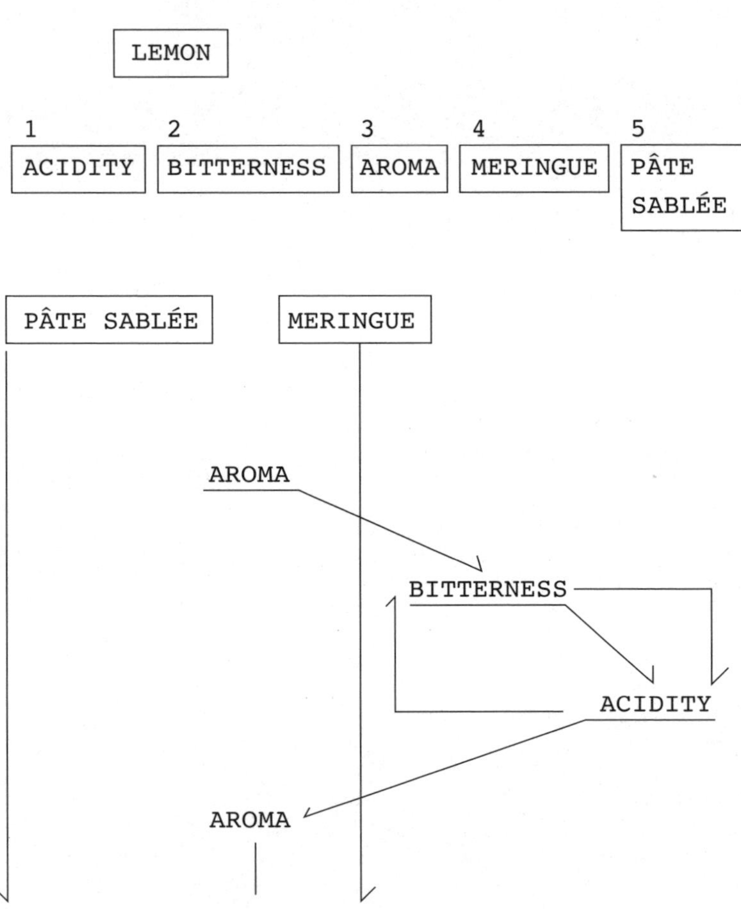

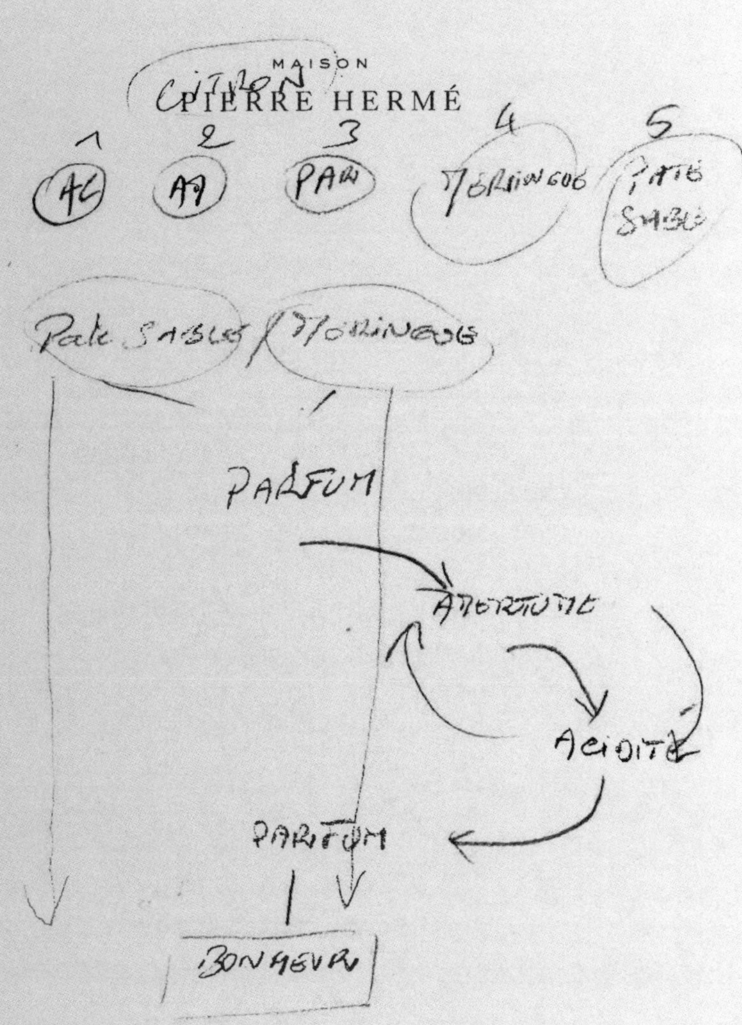
MAISON
PIERRE HERMÉ
12 RUE FORTUNY   PARIS 17e

YASAMINE (p.18)

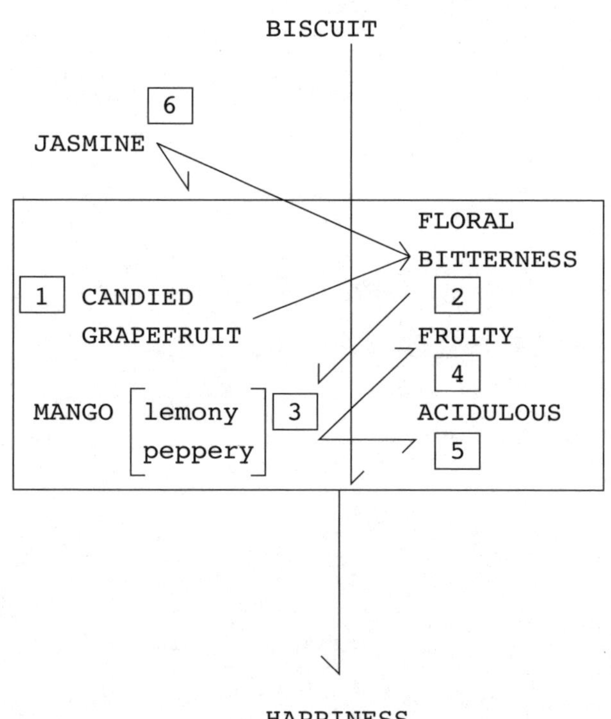

MAISON

PIERRE HERMÉ

<u>PLAISIR SUCRÉ</u> (p. 30)

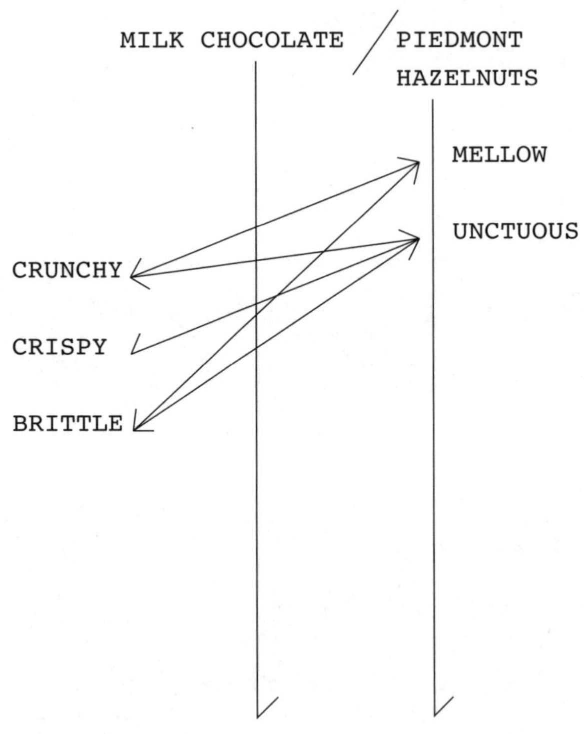

MAISON

PIERRE HERMÉ

PLAISIR SUCRÉ

CHOCOLAT AU LAIT / NOISETTES
DU PIÉMONT

MOELLEUX
ONCTUEUX

CROQUANT

CRAQUANT

CROUSTILLANT

<u>ÉMOTION DÉLICIEUX</u> (p. 38)

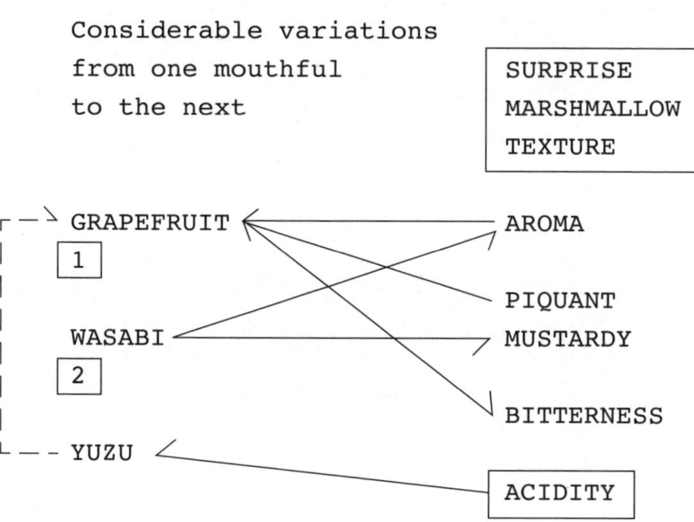

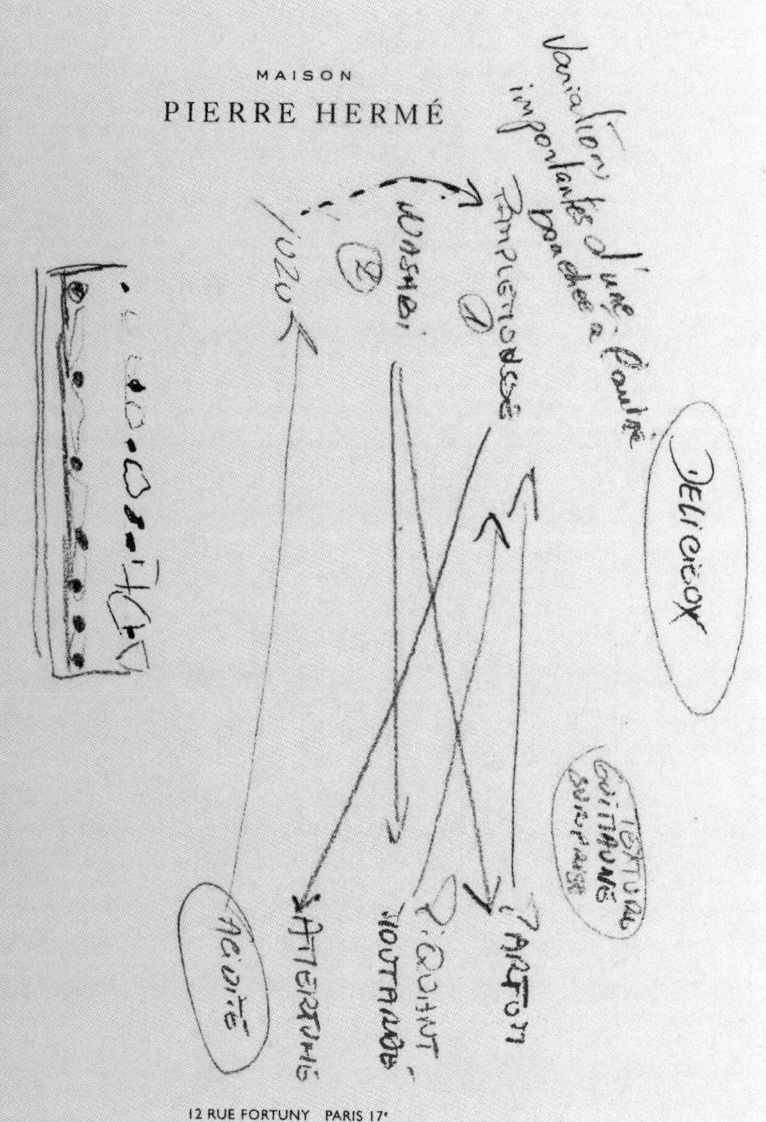

MAISON
PIERRE HERMÉ

12 RUE FORTUNY   PARIS 17e

APPENDIX 2

ENTREMETS INFINIMENT CITRON
Makes 400 pastries

Components
- Semi-candied lemon
- Lemon pâte sablée
- Infiniment Citron meringue
- Infiniment Citron cream
- Infiniment Citron light cream
- Poached lemon gelée
- White chocolate lemon slices

Semi-candied lemon
- 3.2 kg (around 15) lemons
- 2.7 kg mineral water
- 1.35 kg caster sugar
  Total weight: 7.2 kg

Using a serrated knife, remove the ends of the lemon and slice them in quarters from top to bottom. Blanch them three consecutive times: submerge them in a large quantity of boiling water and boil them for two minutes, then rinse them in cold water. Repeat this process two more times and strain them. To prepare the syrup, combine the sugar and water and bring to a boil. Add the lemons and simmer them at a low temperature for around two hours; cover to preserve the lemons' softness. Remove from the flame and macerate overnight before straining with a sieve. Cut them into 5 mm cubes. Store in a sealed container in the refrigerator. Strain them again before using.

Lemon pâte sablée
- 1.8 kg semi-salted extra-fine butter
- 675 g extra-fine butter
- 13 g fleur de sel de Guérande
- 90 g hard-boiled egg yolk (passed through a medium sieve)
- 810 g icing sugar
- 45 g fresh lemon zest
- 2.385 kg flour Type 55 (Viron)
- 450 g potato starch
  Total weight: 6.493 kg

Sift together the flour and potato starch. Temper the butter. In standing mixer with the hook attachment, mix together the ingredients in order until just combined. Wrap it in plastic wrap, and refrigerate on a sheet pan.

Lemon pâte sablée discs
Roll out the pâte sablée to a 2.5 mm thickness using a sheeter. Cut discs of 5.5 cm. Place them on sheet pans lined with parchment, cover with plastic wrap, and store in the freezer.

Baking of lemon pâte sablée discs
- 200 g Mycryo (Cacao Barry)

On sheet pans lined with parchment, place the discs and bake in a convection oven at 165°C for 15 to 18 minutes. Remove from oven and using a strainer dust the discs with Mycryo. Let them cool and keep under film.
NB: After baking, it may be necessary to recut the lemon pâte sablée discs slightly using the circular molds.

Infiniment Citron meringue
- 1.2 kg fresh pasteurized egg whites
- 1.2 kg caster sugar
- 60 g fresh lemon zest
- 1.2 kg caster sugar
  Total weight: 3.66 kg

Using a Microplane grater, zest the lemons in a stainless steel mixing bowl, and rub them with the second quantity of sugar. Place the egg whites in the bowl of a stand mixer. Whisk them at medium speed until they double in volume, while incorporating a quarter of the sugar. Keep whisking until they become very firm, very smooth, and very shiny, while adding the rest of the sugar. Remove the bowl from the mixer and fold in the zest/sugar mixture using a spatula. Use immediately.

Baking of Infiniment Citron meringue
- 200 g Mycryo (Cacao Barry)

Using a piping bag fitted with a #8 tip, pipe the meringue into 5.5 cm wide discs on a sheet pan lined with parchment. Preheat the oven to 120°C, and then lower to 90°C when inserting the sheet pans in the oven. Bake the meringues for 60 to 80 minutes. Allow them to cool; flip the meringue discs delicately, and return to the oven for five minutes. Once out of the oven, dust the discs with Mycryo using a strainer and let them cool completely. Store them at room temperature under film with desiccant packets.

Lemon cream
- 3.78 kg fresh pasteurized eggs
- 4.16 kg caster sugar
- 470 g fresh lemon zest
- 3.025 kg freshly squeezed lemon juice
- 5.67 kg extra-fine butter
  Total weight: 17.105 kg

Using a Microplane grater, zest the lemons in a stainless steel mixing bowl, and rub them with the sugar. Add the eggs and the lemon juice. Poach the mixture in a double bath, stirring occasionally—or use a pasteurizer—until it reaches 83/84°C. Cool it to 60°C using an ice bath or pasteurizer, then whisk in the butter. Mix for 10 minutes using an immersion blender in order to break the molecules of fat to obtain an incredibly unctuous cream. Store in a plastic box and cover the surface of the cream with plastic wrap, letting it cool in the refrigerator for 24 hours before using.

Infiniment Citron cream
- 16 kg lemon cream
- 135 g gelatin sheets Gold Strength (200 Bloom)
  Total weight: 16.135 kg

Bloom the gelatin in ice water for at least 20 minutes. In a saucepan, gently melt the strained gelatin and add a quarter of the lemon cream. In a mixing bowl, mix the rest of the lemon cream with the lemon cream/gelatin mixture. Use immediately.

Infiniment Citron light cream
- 5.15 kg liquid cream (32/34 percent fat)
- 3.43 kg Infiniment Citron cream
  Total weight: 8.58 kg

Using the stand mixer with the whisk attachment, whisk the liquid cream and put aside. In a mixing bowl, mix the Infiniment Citron cream while progressively folding in the whipped cream. Use immediately.

Poached lemon slices
- 5.1 kg mineral water
- 2.55 kg caster sugar
- 3.57 kg sliced lemons
  Total weight: 11.22 kg

Slice the lemons on setting 2 of a meat slicer. Place them in a stainless steel crystallizing tray, no thicker than 1.5 cm. Pour the boiling syrup over the lemons and cover the surface with a film. Allow to macerate for at least 24 hours, then strain it and mince finely using a Robot Coupe.

Poached lemon gelée
- 1.02 kg fresh lemon juice
- 510 g caster sugar
- 2.38 kg poached lemon slices
- 40 g fresh lemon zest
- 44 g gelatin sheets Gold Strength (200 Bloom)
  Total weight: 3.994 kg

Bloom the gelatin in ice water for at least 20 minutes. Heat the lemon juice, the sugar, and the zest to 60°C. Add the strained gelatin and mix. Pour this mixture on the minced poached lemon slices. Use immediately.

Poached lemon gelée cubes
Place a 37 x 57 cm stainless steel frame on a stainless steel sheet lined with plastic film. Pour 2.3 kg of poached lemon gelée in the frame and place in the refrigerator for at least 12 hours. Cut into 1 cm cubes, separate them, and store in the freezer covered in plastic wrap.
NB: 1 frame of 37 x 57 cm = 280/300 pieces.

White chocolate lemon slices
- 1.2 kg couverture Ivoire, 35 percent (Valrhona)
- Printed sheets, lemon diameter 45 mm: lemon slice 75197.101,
  36 cm x 13 cm B1 + J3 (PCB) : 2 boxes PCB
- Custom chablon, lemon diameter 45 mm: 39 mm x 15 mm,
  2 mm, 12 instances per chablon (PCB)

Melt the couverture at 45/50°C in a microwave oven or on a double bath, and temper it. Spread the couverture on a printed sheet covered by the chablon; let it crystallize slightly and remove the chablon. Let crystallize in the fridge and store in a sealed box in the refrigerator.

Assembly
On an aluminum sheet pan lined with a parchment, place circular molds of 6 cm of diameter and 4 cm height, and line them with 3 cm high Rhodoïd strips. Place a disc of lemon pâte sablée at the bottom of each mold, then pipe the Infiniment Citron cream and place the poached lemon gelée cubes and the semi-candied lemon cubes on top. Cover with Infiniment Citron light cream and leave 5 mm to the top of the Rhodoïds. Place the Infiniment Citron meringue discs and press them down lightly. Freeze them for 30 minutes before unfolding and removing the Rhodoïds. Proceed to finishing.
NB: This cake is to be assembled fresh every day.

Finishing
- White chocolate lemon slices

Place a slice of white chocolate lemon flat on top of each pastry.

YASAMINE
Makes 400 pastries

Components
- Jasmine macaron biscuit
- Jasmine cream
- Candied grapefruit
- Seasoned mangos

Titanium dioxide paste
- 200 g titanium dioxide powder
- 100 g mineral water
  Total weight: 300 g

Mix the ingredients and set aside.

"Tant pour tant" almonds
- 4 kg whole white Valencia almonds
- 4 kg "amylacé" icing sugar
  Total weight: 8 kg

Grind the almonds using a Stephan grinder for 45 seconds, then add the icing sugar and keep grinding until very fine.

Jasmine macaron biscuit
To repeat 4 times:
1)
- 2 kg "Tant pour tant" almonds
- 375 g "liquefied" egg whites
- 40 g titanium dioxide paste
2)
- 1 kg caster sugar
- 250 g mineral water
- 375 g "liquefied" egg whites
  Total weight: 4.04 kg

Jasmine macaron biscuit
1)
- 8 kg "Tant pour tant" almonds
- 1.5 kg "liquefied" egg whites
- 160 g titanium dioxide paste
2)
- 4 kg caster sugar
- 1 kg mineral water
- 1.5 kg "liquefied" egg whites
  Total weight: 16.16 kg

Mix the "Tant pour tant" almonds with the first quantity of egg whites and titanium dioxide paste. Cook the sugar and water. When the mix reaches 115°C, start whisking the egg whites in a stand mixer. Let the sugar and water reach 118°C. Once the egg whites are whipped, but not too firm, bring the mixer to speed 2 and pour in the cooked sugar. Let the meringue cool to about 50°C; remove from the mixer. Fold the meringue into the "Tant pour tant" almond, egg white, and titanium dioxide mixture. Allow the paste to lose its volume, then pipe.

Piping of macaron biscuit discs with PH print
- Custom chablon (PCB: round 5.5 cm)
- Printed sheets (PCB: printed sheets 40 x 60 cm round, 5.5 cm PH 75197.100 polyethylene PR12H N10)
- 1 stainless steel triangle

On the work surface, place the printed sheet, then the chablon. Using the stainless steel triangle, cover the sheet evenly with macaron biscuit. Remove the chablon and place the sheet on a hot sheet pan in order to transfer the printing on the macaron biscuit. Let dry at room temperature for 24 hours. Remove the printed macaron discs and use immediately, or store in a box.

Piping and baking
- PH printed macaron biscuit discs

On a parchment-lined sheet pan, pipe macaron shells of 6 cm of diameter using a #11 tip. On the center of each one, place a PH-printed macaron biscuit disc, pushing it down gently, as to create contact on the entire surface of the disc (the macaron will flatten slightly). Leave the macarons to form a crust at room temperature for about 30 minutes. Bake in a convection oven at 165°C for 15 minutes. Always leave the vent open. Remove from the oven and let them cool on the sheet pans. Transfer the shells on wire grates and wrap with plastic film. Store in the refrigerator or freezer.

Italian meringue
1)
- 1.56 kg pasteurized egg whites
- 185 g of caster sugar

2)
- 3.125 kg of caster sugar
- 935 g mineral water
  Total weight: 5.805 kg
  Net weight: 5 kg (need 4.9 kg)

Boil the sugar and the water until it reaches 121°C. At a low speed, whisk the egg whites to soft peaks. When the sugar reaches 115°C, raise the mixer's speed to medium. Pour the cooked sugar (once it reaches 121°C) gently on the whisking egg whites. Let it cool at the same speed.

NB: Once cold, it is preferable to leave the meringue whisking at a low speed, rather than letting it harden. The holding of the result will be better.

Jasmine cream
- 3.34 kg fresh whole milk
- 1.96 kg pasteurized egg yolks
- 1.12 kg caster sugar
- 630 g La Perle de Jade tea - Chine (Cannon tea)

Heat the milk to 75°C, then add the tea and leave to infuse for three minutes (not longer). Strain over the mixed egg yolks and sugar using a chinois, then cook it like a crème anglaise to 85°C and cool in a stand mixer fitted with the whisk attachment at high speed.

NB: This preparation can easily attach to the bottom of the pan during cooking.
- 4.9 kg Italian meringue
- 10.5 kg extra-fine butter, at room temperature
- 210 g jasmine aroma (74 percent Robertet)
  Total weight: 22.96 kg

Cream the butter in the bowl of a stand mixer fitted with the whisk attachment. Add the cooled crème anglaise and mix before folding in the Italian meringue and jasmine aroma with a spatula. Transfer and store in a refrigerator at 4°C.

Candied grapefruit cubes
- 2.27 kg pink grapefruits
- 2.145 kg mineral water (for the syrup)
- 1.07 kg caster sugar
- 110 g freshly squeezed lemon juice
- 4 g star anise (Thiercelin)
- 20 g used vanilla beans
- 4 g freshly ground Sarawak pepper (Thiercelin)
  Total weight: 5.623 kg
  Net weight in cubes: 2.045 kg

Cut off the grapefruit peels, leaving about 1 cm to 1.5 cm of flesh. Blanch the peels in water three times to remove the bitterness. Boil the other ingredients to obtain a syrup, then plunge the grapefruit peels, cover and let them simmer for 1.25 hours to 1.5 hours. Remove from heat and leave it to macerate overnight. Slice into .5 cm cubes, and return them to the syrup and freeze. Strain the night before using them.

Seasoned mangos
- 5 kg of fresh mango cubes
  (or 10 kg of mangos, since 50 percent is discarded)
- 250 g freshly squeezed lime juice
- 50 g freshly grated ginger
  Total weight: 5.3 kg

Peel the fresh ginger and grate using a Microplane grater. Peel the mangos and cut into 1 to 1.5 cm cubes. Delicately mix the ingredients and use immediately or store in the refrigerator.

Assembly
In the bowl of a stand mixer fitted with the whisk attachment, whisk the jasmine cream. Place the macaron shells on the serving plates and let them defrost. Using a piping bag fitted with a #9 tip, pipe balls of jasmine cream along the exterior of the shells. In the center, pipe a thin spiral of jasmine cream and place the candied grapefruit cubes and seasoned mango cubes on top. Cover the fruits with jasmine cream and place the second macaron shell with PH-printed macaron biscuit discs on top. Press down lightly and store in the refrigerator.

PLAISIR SUCRÉ
Makes 400 pastries

Components
- Hazelnut dacquoise
- Hazelnut praliné feuilleté
- Thin sheets of milk chocolate
- Milk chocolate ganache
- Milk chocolate Chantilly cream

Roasted and crushed hazelnuts
- 1 kg whole brown Piedmont hazelnuts
  Total weight: 1 kg

Place the hazelnuts on a parchment-lined sheet pan and roast them at 170°C for about 15 min. Using a sieve, remove the skins and crush them. Store them in a sealed box.

Hazelnut dacquoise
- 1.26 kg Piedmont hazelnut powder
- 1.38 kg icing sugar
- 1.38 kg pasteurized egg whites
- 450 g caster sugar
  Total weight: 4.47 kg

Roast the Piedmont hazelnut powder on a parchment-lined sheet pan at 170°C for about 10 minutes. Sift the icing sugar with the hazelnut powder. In the bowl of a stand mixer, whisk the egg whites while adding the caster sugar in three additions until the meringue is soft. Using a spatula, gently fold in the hazelnut powder and icing sugar. Use immediately.

Baking of the hazelnut dacquoise
Place a 37 x 57 cm frame, 4 cm in height, on a parchment-lined sheet pan. Weigh
1.4 kg of hazelnut dacquoise and spread it evenly within the frame using an offset
spatula. Sprinkle the surface evenly with 200 g of roasted and crushed hazelnuts.
Bake in a convection oven at 170°C for about 35 minutes, leaving the vent open
to prevent the dacquoise to rise and fall because of the steam. Once baked, it
should stay resistant and soft. Once removed from the oven, even the surface
with a large triangle and let cool.

Hazelnut praliné feuilleté
- 900 g hazelnut praliné 65/35 (Valrhona)
- 900 g pure Piedmont hazelnut paste (Fugar)
- 450 g Hermé milk couverture, 45 percent (Valrhona)
- 900 g Eclats d'or (Valrhona)
- 180 g extra-fine butter
  Total weight: 3.33 kg

Melt the butter and couverture separately at 40/45°C over a double bath. Using
the paddle attachment of the stand mixer, mix the hazelnut praliné, the pure
hazelnut paste, and the melted couverture and butter. Add the Eclats d'or and
use immediately.

Hazelnut dacquoise and praliné feuilleté frames
Weigh 1.1 kg of praliné feuilleté and spread evenly on top of the hazelnut
dacquoise frames using a spatula (palette coudée). Store in the refrigerator.

Cutting of hazelnut dacquoise and praliné feuilleté frames
Cut the hazelnut dacquoise and praliné feuilleté frames into 5 x 2.5 cm
rectangles. Store in the refrigerator.
NB: There are around 150 pieces per frame.

Thin sheets of milk chocolate
- 5 kg Hermé milk couverture, 45 percent (Valrhona) tempered

Spread 320 g of Hermé couverture on a 40 x 60 cm sheet of Rhodoïd film. As soon
as the couverture sets, cut into 5 x 2.5 cm rectangles. Cover with a parchment
sheet and a sheet pan and let crystalize in the refrigerator.
NB: Three rectangles per pastry; 40 rectangles of 5 x 2.5 cm = 100 g

Milk chocolate ganache
- 2.15 kg liquid cream (32/34 percent fat)
- 2.435 kg Hermé milk couverture, 45 percent (Valrhona)
  Total weight: 4.585 kg

Chop the couverture. Bring the cream to a boil and pour on the couverture. Mix
with a whisk, starting from the center toward the sides. Pour into a stainless steel

crystallizing tray and cover the surface with plastic wrap. Let cool and set at room temperature for few hours. Do not store in refrigerator.

Assembly of the thin chocolate sheets and of milk chocolate ganache
Place the thin sheets of milk chocolate on a parchment-lined sheet pan (shiny side down). Using a piping bag fitted with a railway tip, cover the chocolate rectangles, piping from side to side along the length with milk chocolate ganache. Superimpose with a second sheet of chocolate, and repeat. Do not add a third chocolate sheet on top of the second layer of ganache. Set in the refrigerator, then store in the freezer.

Milk chocolate chantilly cream
- 5.3 kg liquid cream (32/34 percent fat)
- 3.7 kg Hermé milk couverture, 45 percent (Valrhona)
  Total weight: 9 kg

Chop the couverture. Bring the cream to a boil and pour on the couverture. Mix with a whisk, starting from the center toward the sides. Pour into a stainless steel crystallizing tray and cover the surface with plastic wrap. Let it cool for about 12 hours in the refrigerator. This cream can be frozen as is.

Assembly and finishing
In the bowl of a stand mixer fitted with the whisk attachment, whisk the milk chocolate Chantilly cream. Place it in a piping bag fitted with a #12 tip. On each hazelnut dacquoise and praliné feuilleté rectangle, pipe a line of milk chocolate Chantilly cream. On top, place a rectangle of milk chocolate and milk chocolate ganache. Pipe two lines of milk chocolate Chantilly cream from side to side. Finish by placing a thin sheet of milk chocolate (shiny side up). In the middle of the milk chocolate rectangle, place a small round PH logo with milk chocolate Chantilly cream.
NB: Do not try to whip the milk chocolate Chantilly cream without letting it cool at least 12 hours in the refrigerator; it might become grainy.

ÉMOTION DÉLICIEUX
Makes 400 pastries

Components
- Joconde biscuit
- Wasabi gelée
- Fresh and candied grapefruit cubes
- Wasabi mascarpone cream
- Matcha green tea marshmallows

Joconde biscuit
- 600 g pasteurized eggs
- 440 g ground almonds
- 360 g "amylacé" icing sugar
- 12 g Facil'Cake emulsifier (Marguerite)
- 100 g liquid sorbitol
- 40 g inverted sugar (Trimoline)
- 120 g flour Type 55 (Viron)
- 80 g extra-fine butter
- 380 g "liquefied" egg whites
- 60 g caster sugar
  Total weight: 2.192 kg

In the bowl of a stand mixer fitted with the whisk attachment, mix the ground almonds, Trimoline, emulsifier, sorbitol, and the icing sugar. Add half of the eggs and whisk for eight minutes, then add the remaining eggs in two additions and whisk for an additional 10 to 12 minutes. Pour a bit of this mixture in the butter and whisk. Make a meringue with the egg whites and caster sugar and fold it into the first mixture. Sift the flour on top and fold delicately before incorporating the butter. Use immediately.

Sheets and discs of joconde biscuit
Place a 2 mm high frame for joconde on a Silpat. Using a spatula (palette coudée), spread 530 g of the biscuit dough. Bake in a convection oven at 230°C for five to six minutes. Flip it onto a parchment sheet and remove the Silpat. Using a round cutter, cut out 35 mm diameter discs. Store the discs in the freezer.

Wasabi gelée
- 8 kg mineral water
- 3.2 kg sweet yuzu juice
- 1.6 kg caster sugar
- 160 g gelatin sheets Gold Strength (200 Bloom)
- 800 g finely grated fresh wasabi root
  Total weight: 13.76 kg
  Net weight: 13.12 kg

Peel the wasabi roots and put them in the freezer. Process them through a Robot
Coupe to reduce them to a fine paste. Bloom the gelatin sheets in ice water for
at least 20 minutes. In a stainless steel saucepan, heat the yuzu juice to 50°C.
Strain the gelatin and incorporate it into the yuzu juice. Mix it with a whisk, then
pour it on top of the mineral water, the caster sugar, and fresh wasabi paste, and
mix. Use immediately, or store it in a 4°C refrigerator in a sealed plastic box.
NB: You can also grate the wasabi with a special shark-skin grater.

Freshly peeled grapefruit
  • 30 kg pink grapefruits
Using a well-sharpened knife, chop off the ends of the grapefruits and, in a top
down motion following the shape of the fruit, remove the peel of the grapefruits
so as to leave the flesh exposed. Remove the segments.

Segments of grapefruit
  • Desired quantity of grapefruits
Starting with the peeled grapefruit, remove the segments using a paring knife.
Depending on the size of the segments, cut in three or four pieces across the
length. Store in a sealed box in the refrigerator.

Candied grapefruit cubes
  • 6.36 kg pink grapefruits
  • 6 kg mineral water (for the syrup)
  • 3 kg caster sugar
  • 300 g freshly squeezed lemon juice
  • 12 g star anise (Thiercelin)
  • 60 g used vanilla beans
  • 12 g freshly ground Sarawak pepper (Thiercelin)
    Total weight: 15.744 kg
    Net weight in cubes: 5.73 kg
Cut off the grapefruit the peels, leaving about 1 cm to 1.5 cm of flesh. Blanch the
peels in water three times to remove the bitterness. Boil the other ingredients
to obtain a syrup, then plunge the grapefruit peels, cover and let them simmer
for 1.25 hours to 1.5 hours. Remove from heat and leave it to macerate overnight.
Slice into .5 cm cubes, and return them to the syrup and freeze. Strain the night
before using them.

Fresh and candied grapefruit cubes
  • 13 kg fresh grapefruit cubes
  • 5.2 kg candied grapefruit cubes
    Total weight: 18.2 kg
Mix together and use immediately, or store in the refrigerator.

Wasabi crème anglaise
- 10 kg liquid cream (32/34 percent fat)
- 2 kg pasteurized egg yolks
- 2.5 kg caster sugar
- 140 g gelatin sheets Gold Strength (200 Bloom)
- 1.5 kg finely grated fresh wasabi roots
  Total weight: 16.14 kg
  Net weight: 15.04 kg

Peel the wasabi roots and put them in the freezer. Process them through a Robot Coupe to reduce them to a fine paste. Bloom the gelatin sheets in ice water for at least 20 minutes. In a stainless steel saucepan, heat the heavy cream. Mix the egg yolks with the caster sugar. Pour a part of the liquid cream on the blanched egg yolks and cook like a classic crème anglaise to 85°C. Strain the gelatin and incorporate it into the cooked crème anglaise, add the finely grated fresh wasabi roots. Mix. Transfer to a crystallizing tray or sealed box with plastic wrap on the surface, and store in a 4°C refrigerator.
NB: You can also grate the wasabi with a special shark-skin grater.

Wasabi mascarpone cream
- 13.2 kg wasabi crème anglaise
- 8.8 kg mascarpone (Galbani)
  Total weight: 22 kg

In the bowl of a stand mixer fitted with the whisk attachment, beat the mascarpone to homogenize it. Add the wasabi crème anglaise in three rounds, and whisk together. Use immediately.

Matcha green tea marshmallows
- 2 kg caster sugar
- 600 g mineral water (1)
- 80 g glucose syrup
- 60 g matcha green tea
- 720 g mineral water (2)
- 80 g gelatin sheets Gold Strength (200 Bloom)
- 320 g pasteurized egg whites
- 8 g fleur de sel de Guérande
  Total weight: 3.868 kg

Bloom the gelatin in ice water for at least 20 minutes. In a stainless steel saucepan, cook the sugar with the water (1) and the glucose to 117°C. Mix the matcha green tea, the lukewarm water (2), and the strained gelatin. Pour the cooked sugar on the meringue and incorporate the previous mixture. Let it cool at medium speed.

Shaping of the matcha green tea marshmallows
- 500 g cornstarch
- 500 g icing sugar

Sift together the cornstarch and icing sugar. On a Silpat outfitted with a
37 x 57 cm stainless steel frame, 1 cm of height, spread 2 kg of matcha green
tea marshmallows. Dust the surface lightly with the cornstarch-icing sugar
mixture and let it dry overnight, in a 25°C dry room. The following day, flip
the marshmallow and repeat the operation, letting it dry overnight in a 25°C
dry room.

Cutting of the matcha green tea marshmallows
Cut the rectangles of matcha green tea marshmallows in 1.2 cm cubes. Dust
very lightly with the cornstarch-icing sugar mixture before sifting them to
remove superfluous dusting. Store in a sealed box in a dry place.

Assembly
- Wasabi gelée
- Joconde biscuit
- Wasabi mascarpone cream
- Fresh and candied grapefruit cubes

Pour 30 g of wasabi gelée in an "Emotion" glass. Let it set in the refrigerator
and place a 35 mm disc of joconde biscuit. Top with 45 g of fresh and candied
grapefruit cubes. Using a disposable piping bag fitted with a 12 mm tip, pipe 55 g
of wasabi mascarpone cream. Refrigerate.

Finishing
Irregularly place six to seven matcha green tea marshmallow cubes on the wasabi
mascarpone cream.

PIERRE HERMÉ
The Architecture of Taste

Published by the Harvard University Graduate School of Design
and Sternberg Press

ISBN 978-3-95679-139-0

20 19 18 17   2 3 4 5

HARVARD UNIVERSITY
GRADUATE SCHOOL OF DESIGN
48 QUINCY STREET
CAMBRIDGE, MA 02138
GSD.HARVARD.EDU

STERNBERG PRESS
CAROLINE SCHNEIDER
KARL-MARX-ALLEE 78
D-10243 BERLIN
STERNBERG-PRESS.COM

PIERRE HERMÉ is heir to four generations of Alsatian bakery and pastry-making tradition, and began his career at the age of 14 as an apprentice to Gaston Lenôtre. Hermé has since gone on to revolutionize pastry-making; he has invented a unique world of tastes, sensations, and pleasures that can be discovered at Pierre Hermé Paris boutiques around the world. Created in 1997, the Maison is now present in Europe, Asia, and the Middle East; is a member of the Comité Colbert; and has established partnerships with the Raffles and Ritz Carlton groups.

SAVINIEN CARACOSTEA is a creative director, writer, editor, and consultant. He has degrees in architecture from the Harvard University Graduate School of Design and Cornell University, and a degree in pastry arts from the French Culinary Institute. He is a partner of the creative agency AtelierSlice.

SANFORD KWINTER is Professor of Science and Design at Pratt Institute, New York, and University Professor of Theory at the University of Applied Arts, Vienna. His recent books include *Far From Equilibrium: Essays on Technology and Design Culture* (Actar, 2008) and *Requiem: For the City at the End of the Millennium* (Actar, 2010).